Millard Fillmore

Millard Fillmore

Dan Santow

AMERICA'S
13 TH
PRESIDENT

Children's Press®
A Division of Scholastic Inc.
New York / Toronto / London / Auckland / Sydney
Mexico City / New Delhi / Hong Kong
Danbury, Connecticut

Library of Congress Cataloging-in-Publication Data

Santow, Dan.
       Millard Fillmore / by Dan Santow.
          p. cm. — (Encyclopedia of presidents. Second series)
          Summary: A biography of the thirteenth president of the United States,
with information about his childhood, family, political career, presidency, and
legacy.
Includes bibliographical references and index.
  ISBN 0-516-22888-9
   1. Fillmore, Millard, 1800–1874—Juvenile literature. 2. Presidents—United
States—Biography—Juvenile literature. [1. Fillmore, Millard, 1800–1874. 2.
Presidents.] I. Title. II. Series.
E427.S27 2003
973.6'4'092—dc22   2003015937

CHILDREN'S PRESS and associated logos are trademarks and or registered
trademarks of Scholastic Library Publishing. SCHOLASTIC and associated
logos are trademarks and or registered trademarks of Scholastic Inc.
1 2 3 4 5 6 7 8 9 10 R 13 12 11 10 09 08 07 06 05 04

Contents

Chapter 1

A Sleepless Night ——————————————

Millard Fillmore was not the sort of man to lose sleep. He was a sound sleeper who looked forward to waking each morning rested and ready to work.

This hot July night was different, however. For the first time in years, he lay awake in his bed staring at the ceiling. He was alone in his Washington, D.C., residence. His wife Abigail and their two children were away to escape the oppressive heat and humidity. Only a short time ago he had learned that President Zachary Taylor had died after an unexpected illness. As vice president, Fillmore would be sworn in as president the following day—July 10, 1850—at noon.

Fillmore later wrote that he spent much of that night thinking about his life, and how he'd gotten to this position. It had been a long road, full of twists and surprises. He also thought about the country he

General Zachary Taylor, who became president in March 1849 and died in office after a short illness in July 1850.

was to lead. It was in serious trouble, torn by emotional and sometimes violent arguments over slavery and states' rights. As president, he knew he would be forced to make some difficult choices that were sure to anger friends and enemies alike. The awesome responsibility was difficult to accept. He had disagreed with President Taylor about many things, but now he began to realize the heavy burden the old president must have felt.

The series of events that led to Fillmore's sleepless night began on the Fourth of July. The nation's capital was bright and gleaming. The skies were blue and the mood festive. A parade snaked through the city, with marching bands playing patriotic songs. The American flag, with its 30 stars representing the 30 states in the Union, was everywhere.

At the site of the Washington Monument, not far from the Capitol building, a ceremony was planned. The project had been approved two years earlier, and work was only now getting under way. The huge column, rising 550 feet (168 meters) above the capital city would not be finished for nearly 40 years, but the site was already a symbolic meeting place for the nation.

President Taylor was there to listen to long patriotic speeches and greet citizens celebrating the national holiday. In spite of the heat, Taylor was wearing a heavy black wool suit with a stiff high collar. When it came time for him to turn over a shovelful of dirt to begin construction, Taylor did more than his share, digging a big hole as spectators watched and applauded.

When the celebrations came to an end, the president took a long walk in the midday heat along the Potomac River before returning to the White House. He was hot and tired and drenched in sweat. At the White House, Taylor cooled himself by eating a bowl of chilled cherries and drinking a large pitcher of cold milk. Before long, he had severe cramps in his stomach and soon developed a high fever.

Over the next few days the president got worse. Doctors bustled around him and prescribed the medicines and treatments then available, but nothing seemed to help. By noon on July 8, Taylor was so ill that Fillmore was called out of the Senate chamber, where he was presiding over another tense debate, to go to Taylor's sickbed. For the first time, Fillmore realized that Taylor might die of his illness. "In all likelihood," wrote one historian, during these hours Fillmore was "numb with disbelief."

On the evening of July 9, Taylor called his wife to him and asked her not to weep. "I have always done my duty, I am ready to die." he told her. "My only regret is for the friends I leave behind me." Not long afterward, President Taylor died.

"I have no language to express the emotions of my heart," said Fillmore upon receiving the news from a messenger. "The shock is so sudden and unexpected that I am overwhelmed."

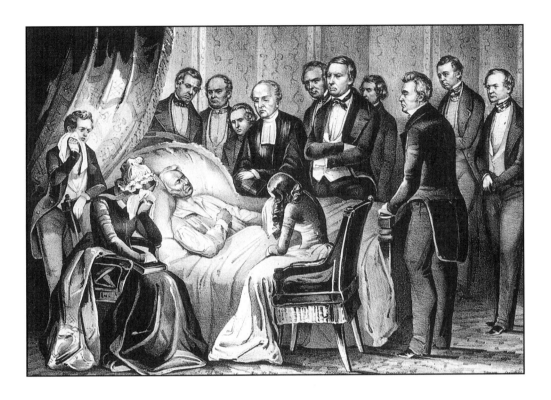

An artist's impression of Zachary Taylor's deathbed scene. Vice President Millard Fillmore is at the center right with his arms crossed. In reality, he was not at the White House when President Taylor died.

A Mourning Nation ———————————

Most presidents take office in an atmosphere filled with hope. An inaugural ceremony attracts thousands of supporters. Inaugural parties last late into the night. Fillmore took office when the country was still in shock and mourning over President Taylor's death. There would be no celebrations. With his wife Abigail and their children still away, Fillmore could not even turn to his family for comfort.

He was sworn in at noon in the House chamber before both houses of Congress by Judge William Cranch.

"I appeal to you to aid me under the trying circumstances which surround me, in the discharge of my duties, from which, however much I may be oppressed

"Old Rough-and-Ready"

Zachary Taylor was a career officer in the United States Army, and he also owned cotton plantations and dozens of slaves. In 1846 and 1847, he won a series of battles in Texas and northern Mexico during the U.S.-Mexican War that made him a national hero. In 1848, he was nominated by the Whig party to run for president. With Millard Fillmore as his vice presidential running mate, Taylor was elected in November and took office in March 1849.

Taylor, who had never held an elective office before, entered the White House at a difficult time. Arguments between northern and southern politicians about slavery, especially in the new territories gained from Mexico during the war, threatened to divide the nation in two.

Taylor offered a *compromise* plan that he hoped both sides could agree to. In Congress, Senator Henry Clay (also a Whig) offered a more ambitious plan and criticized the president's proposal. As the Whig president and the most powerful Whig congressman quarreled, Congress remained deadlocked, unable to agree on any compromise at all.

Then Taylor died after only 16 months in office. Millard Fillmore was left to wrestle with the issues that were dividing both his party and the nation.

☆★☆

Millard Fillmore as he looked when he became president in July 1850.

by them, I dare not shrink," Fillmore said, "and I rely upon Him who holds in His hands the destinies of nations to endow me with the requisite strength for the task, and to avert from our country the evils apprehended from the heavy calamity which has befallen us."

Three days later, 100,000 people watched solemnly as eight white horses accompanied by grooms wearing white turbans led the hearse which carried President Taylor's body through the streets of Washington. It was followed by other dignitaries, military units, the president's loyal horse Old Whitey, and the president's family. Behind them a line of officials and common citizens stretched in procession for more than two miles (3 kilometers). Taylor's body was later buried in Louisville, Kentucky, where he had grown up.

When Fillmore and his family moved into the White House, its rooms were draped with black cloth as a sign of mourning for President Taylor. The atmosphere was somber, and the mood throughout the country was one of confusion and sadness. Not only was the president dead, but the country itself was divided, and its own future seemed to be in question.

Fillmore had many conflicting feelings. He felt the weight of responsibility for leading the country at a time of crisis and uncertainty. Yet he was also amazed at the turn of events. He had come so far in life!

Chapter 2

A Log Cabin Childhood ——————

In 1800, at the dawn of a new century, life was hard in the densely forested region of central New York State. Farmers cleared their land, removing huge old trees, only to discover that the clay-filled soil was poor. There were small settlements and isolated farms connected by a handful of dirt roads and pathways. Wolves and bears roamed the land. The weather was frigid in winter and blisteringly hot in summer.

One of the settlers in this territory was Nathaniel Fillmore. He had arrived in 1799 with his wife Phoebe and a young daughter from the "stone-strewn lands" of Bennington, Vermont, even farther north. They claimed land in Locke Township, New York, and hoped to make a better life.

On January 7, 1800, the Fillmores' second child was born. He was named Millard, which was his mother's maiden name. The family lived in a log cabin that Nathaniel had built, more than four miles (6 km) from their nearest neighbor. Nathaniel and Phoebe were too poor to buy a crib for their newborn, so Millard slept in a trough normally used to collect syrup from the maple trees that dotted the land.

It gradually became clear to Nathaniel that the land he'd chosen would never be fertile enough to feed his growing family, so he moved to land near Sempronius, a few miles to the northeast. Meanwhile, the family grew. Millard would eventually have five brothers and three sisters.

When Millard turned six, he had his first chance to go to school, in a nearby town called New Hope, where he sat on a backless bench in the one-room schoolhouse and learned the alphabet. His stay there was brief, though. There were no free public schools, so schooling cost money. Besides, Millard's father needed his children for work on the farm. Throughout the rest of his boyhood, Millard went to school only occasionally, for a few weeks or months at a time. In between, he followed a routine of hard work, learning the tasks of a farmer.

"During that time," Fillmore wrote many years later, "being large of my age and unusually strong, I learned to plow, to hoe, to chop, to log and clear land, to mow, to reap, and finally to do all kinds of work which is usually done in clearing and cultivating a new farm." It was backbreaking work for a grown man, let alone a boy. Nathaniel Fillmore didn't allow time for play. Millard wrote, "He

A replica of the log cabin in which Fillmore was born in 1800 in Cayuga County, New York.

used to tell me that no man ever prospered who spent much of his time hunting and fishing."

Millard did make friends with some boys his age. According to one historian, he was "the acknowledged favorite of his young companions." It was said that Millard was "often chosen arbiter of their little disputes, which he seldom failed to settle in a manner entirely satisfactory. From his earliest childhood, he was remarkable for these peaceable traits of disposition."

From an early age, Millard showed a desire to succeed beyond the family farm, to do good, and to see the world. When news of the War of 1812 reached the region, twelve-year-old Millard asked his father if he could volunteer to fight. Of course his father refused, but it did get him thinking about his oldest son's future.

Learning a Trade

Nathaniel Fillmore found that it was difficult to feed his family even if he worked at his farm chores around the clock. If it was that way for him, he thought, it would be that way for his children, too, so he discouraged them from farming. He called it "the meanest [lowest] of occupations." When Millard turned 14, an age at which boys of that era frequently began to support themselves, his father arranged for Millard to take apprenticeship with a cloth-dresser in the town of Sparta, New York, more than 100 miles (160 km) to the west. Cloth-dressers

The War of 1812

In September 1814, near the end of the War of 1812, the U.S. Navy destroyed a British fleet on Lake Champlain near Plattsburgh, New York. Fillmore was 14 years old.

The War of 1812, between the United States and Great Britain, was important news in Fillmore's boyhood home. U.S. soldiers invaded British Canada across the Niagara River in western New York State, and captured York (present-day Toronto). The next year, British troops invaded New York and burned the town of Buffalo. Late in the war, the British tried to invade again, sailing down Lake Champlain, in the northeast. They were stopped by a U.S. force near the town of Plattsburgh, New York, and forced to return to Canada.

The war was ended by a treaty in December 1814, but before the news reached the United States, a British force marched on New Orleans in Louisiana. They were stopped and driven back by Americans commanded by Andrew Jackson. Helped by his military fame, Jackson was twice elected president. He was in the White House when Millard Fillmore first took his seat in the U.S. House of Representatives.

processed sheeps' wool into woolen cloth for making clothing and blankets. Millard's father thought that learning the trade of cloth-making would allow Millard to earn a good living. (He also received a fee from the cloth-maker for apprenticing his son.)

In Sparta, the cloth-maker, Benjamin Hungerford, turned out to be a stern and unforgiving master. In addition, Millard was lonely. He had never spent more than two days away from his family and now he was alone in a strange place all by himself, working from dawn to dusk. He complained that at home he could eat whatever was available whenever he chose, but in the Hungerford house, "I was compelled to eat boiled salt pork, which I detested . . . and buckwheat cakes, or starve."

Even though Millard had been sent there to learn how to dress cloth, Hungerford instead made him chop wood for the coal pit. He was working hard, Millard thought, but learning little. "I became exceedingly sore under this servitude," Fillmore wrote.

One day, after he'd been chopping wood for many hours, he returned tired and achy to the shop, only to be confronted by Hungerford and told to return to the woodpile. "I took up my ax, and said (perhaps not very respectfully) that I did not come there to learn to chop," Fillmore wrote, "and immediately left without waiting for a reply."

Fillmore was apprenticed to learn the trade of cloth-dressing — making and finishing wool from the fleece of sheep. He worked in small shops or mills like this one.

Hungerford followed Millard up the hill and asked Millard if he thought he was being mistreated. "I was burning with indignation," Millard wrote, "and felt keenly the injustice and insult, and said to him, 'You will not chastise me': and, raising my ax, said, 'if you approach me I will split you down.'" Hungerford walked away, and soon afterward Millard walked away, too, more than 100 miles home through the forests and farms. He had lived in Sparta less than four months.

It had been a terrible experience, a lonely time, but in later years Fillmore reflected that while he learned little about cloth-making, he had learned something else. "I think this injustice—which was no more than other apprentices have suffered and will suffer—had a marked effect on my character," he wrote later. "It made me feel for the weak and unprotected and hate the insolent tyrant in every station of life."

Discovering Books

Soon after Millard returned home, his father arranged another apprenticeship for him at a cloth mill in the nearby town of New Hope. There, Millard said, he became "painfully aware" of his ignorance, of how little education he had. Though he could read, there wasn't much *to* read. The Fillmore family library consisted of a Bible, a hymnbook, and an almanac.

While at his new apprenticeship, Millard was able to attend some school during slow periods at the mill. When he was 17, a small library was established and Millard began to read as much as he could and as often as possible. He soon realized how few words he really understood! So he saved his money and bought a dictionary. He was, he said, "determined to seek out the meaning of every word occurring in my reading which I did not understand."

Millard's determination to learn was so dogged that he carried the dictionary to the mill. He leaned it against a desk so that he could read a definition when he passed by between chores. "In this way I could have a moment in which to look at a word and read its definition, and could then fix it in my memory," he wrote. "This I found quite successful."

At school, one of his teachers was 21-year-old Abigail Powers, whose father had been a Baptist minister. He died when Abigail was only two years old but left a home filled with books. Abigail had been taught mainly by her mother and started teaching when she was 16 to help support herself and to continue her own education. Millard admired her interest in teaching others and learning more herself. She also had a fair complexion and light auburn hair, which she wore in a tight bun. Millard began courting her.

Eyes on the Law

Nathaniel Fillmore saw that Millard was succeeding in school and was eager to make something of himself. Nathaniel visited the man he rented farmland from, a wealthy judge and landowner named Walter Wood. Nathaniel asked Judge Wood to hire Millard as a law clerk. When Millard heard from his mother what his father had done, "the news was so unexpected and sudden that, in spite of myself, I burst out crying, and had to leave the table, much mortified at my weakness."

Millard took up the clerkship and worked hard to please the judge and to learn as much as he could while there. He began to hope that he might become a lawyer by studying with Judge Wood. The problem was that the clerkship offered no pay. He had taken a break from his apprenticeship and had to decide whether to go back to the cloth mill.

"If you have an ambition for distinction and can sacrifice everything else to success, the law is the road that leads to honors," the judge told Millard, "and if you can get rid of your engagement to serve as an apprentice, I would advise you to come back again and study law."

Millard decided to take the chance. He arranged to end his apprenticeship and continued to study with Judge Wood. To earn money, he taught school and did odd jobs. For the first time, Millard felt he was making progress. He had grown to be a strapping young man, six feet (1.8 m) tall with broad shoulders and a pink complexion. He gave up wearing cowhide boots and began to wear proper shoes and suits with white collared shirts.

In 1821, in an attempt to make an extra three dollars, Millard agreed to represent a farmer in a case before a local justice of the peace. When Judge Wood learned of this, he and Millard argued. The judge said that Millard was too

The small city of Buffalo, with its harbor on Lake Erie, about the time the Fillmore family moved to the nearby village of East Aurora in 1821. The city had been burned by the British during the War of 1812.

inexperienced to take on such duties. Millard disagreed. He and the judge parted company. Millard's family had moved again, this time traveling more than 200 miles (320 km) west to East Aurora, New York, near the growing town of Buffalo. Millard packed his bags and walked the long road to East Aurora.

Millard soon found another law clerkship in East Aurora. The lawyers, Asa Rice and Joseph Clary, were so impressed with Millard's intelligence and diligence that they soon persuaded the authorities to allow Millard to practice law before the traditional seven years of training were finished. From his birth in a dirt-floored log cabin, he had risen to be a lawyer.

One day in 1825, Abigail arrived in East Aurora for a visit. The two had been writing to each other, but hadn't met for more than three years. Millard asked Abigail to marry him, and she agreed. They traveled back to the old neighborhood in central New York, where they were married on February 5, 1826, at Abigail's brother's home in Moravia, New York.

They settled in East Aurora, and Millard set out to build a law practice. To make ends meet, Abigail continued to teach. It was very rare for a woman to work outside the home after her marriage. Fillmore gained a reputation as honest and hardworking, and he was soon earning a living.

Chapter 3

First Campaigns

In June 1828, Fillmore got his first taste of politics. The National Republicans of Erie County met in Buffalo to consider the party's presidential candidates. The majority of the delegates, including Fillmore, endorsed President John Quincy Adams for reelection. Even though Adams and the National Republicans lost the election, party leaders noticed Fillmore as a young man with a future.

The next month, Fillmore attended another political convention, that of the recently formed Anti-Masonic party. The Freemasons were members of a lodge, an organization of men who met to enjoy each other's company and discuss important affairs of the day. The Masons' organization and ceremonies were secret, and members pledged never to reveal them to outsiders. In the 1820s, Masonic lodge members included many influential merchants and political leaders.

The house in East Aurora, New York, where Millard and Abigail Fillmore lived in the late 1820s. Today it is a Fillmore museum.

In 1826, a former Mason named William Morgan, from Batavia, New York, announced that he had written a book that revealed the Masonic secrets and rituals. Members of the lodge were outraged that Morgan had violated their trust. He was arrested on a charge that he refused to pay a debt of only three dollars and imprisoned. An angry mob of Masons and their sympathizers gathered outside the prison. The sheriff released Morgan to the waiting mob. Morgan was carried off to an abandoned fort. Then he disappeared and was never seen again.

This sensational case raised a huge outcry among non-Masons, who believed Morgan had been kidnapped and murdered for revealing the lodge's secrets. The Anti-Masonic party was formed to break the hold influential Masons had in politics. One of the organizers was Thurlow Weed, a young newspaperman who would play an influential role in Millard Fillmore's life. Weed began a newspaper called the *Anti-Masonic Enquirer* and used it to support the party's viewpoint. In 1828, Weed and others in the party encouraged Fillmore to run for the New York State Assembly seat representing Erie County. He ran and won his election handily. He was reelected in 1829 and 1830.

As the assemblyman from Erie Country, Fillmore took an active role in the state assembly. One of the issues he addressed was the imprisonment of debtors. In those days an individual who could not pay a debt could be put into prison until the debt was paid. Fillmore thought the practice was wrong and

Political Conventions

Local political conventions in Fillmore's time were the gatherings where political parties actually chose candidates for the general election. In 1831, the Anti-Masonic party held the first national convention to nominate candidates for president and vice president. Until that time, presidential candidates for other parties were nominated by the party's members in Congress or by state legislatures. The Anti-Masonic convention gained so much attention, however, that soon the major parties took up the idea. From the 1830s to the 1950s national conventions nominated the candidates for all major parties.

Beginning in the 1950s, a system of primary elections allowed ordinary members of a political party to vote for the presidential candidates they prefer. Delegates to a national convention are required to support the candidate preferred by the voters in their state. National conventions continue, but by the time they meet, the choice of the party's presidential candidates has usually been made in the primary elections.

☆ ☆ ☆

worked to end it. He had the support of the governor, Enos Throop, who said, "The notion of imprisonment, in the nature of punishment for debt, is repugnant to humanity, and condemned by wisdom." Fillmore also sponsored legislation supporting public education.

In 1830 the Fillmores moved from East Aurora to Buffalo, where they purchased a house surrounded by a white picket fence. The house sat on a hill, and from it, Fillmore could see the tall masts of ships in nearby Lake Erie.

The old Capitol building in Albany, New York, where Fillmore served as a state legislator.

Buffalo had 8,600 people and was growing rapidly. The city was at the western end of the Erie Canal, which transported goods and people from Lake Erie across New York State to the Hudson River and the Atlantic, and it was becoming an important city for business and industry.

Millard and Abigail developed an active social life, hosting formal dinners and attending chamber music concerts, dances, and lectures. As former teachers, they were avid collectors of books. Their library eventually grew to more than 4,000 titles! They also became active members in the Unitarian Church. The Fillmores' son Millard Powers was two years old when they moved to Buffalo in 1830, and in 1832, their daughter Mary Abigail (nicknamed Abby) was born.

Fillmore traveled across the state to Albany, the state capital, for sessions of the state assembly, which met for four months each year. The rest of the year, Fillmore began to build a successful law practice in Buffalo. His greatest ability was that he knew how to get things done. As one historian wrote, "He was not a showman, but rather a citizen-in-office, and about him was always an aura of dignity."

In 1832, at the end of his third one-year term in the state assembly, the Anti-Masonic party approached him to run for a seat in the U.S. House of Representatives, and he agreed. Again he easily won election, this time with support from both Anti-Masonic and National Republican party voters.

Political Parties

Political parties have been an important part of the political process since the early days of the American republic. In 1800, the Democratic-Republican party established by Thomas Jefferson and James Madison won its first election, defeating John Adams, the candidate of the Federalist party.

After 1816, the Federalist party lost support and melted away, leaving only the Democratic-Republicans. They splintered into several groups, which gradually formed into new parties. Millard Fillmore supported the National Republicans in the 1820s. Like the early Federalists, National Republicans favored a strong "national" government that would improve roads and canals and would help American businesses succeed. Another splinter of the old Democratic-Republican party took the name Democratic Party. It reelected President Andrew Jackson in 1832 and elected Martin Van Buren in 1836.

Soon afterward, National Republicans and unhappy Democrats joined together to form the Whig Party, which was devoted to opposing the policies and actions of Andrew Jackson. Fillmore joined the Whigs soon after their founding. They elected their first president, William Henry Harrison, in 1840. In 1848, Fillmore himself would be on the Whigs' national ticket.

The Democratic party remains one of two major parties to this day. The Whig party disappeared during the 1850s, divided over the issue of slavery. Soon the Republican party became the new major party, campaigning to stop the spread of slavery. Ever since, the Democrats and Republicans have remained the major parties in American politics.

☆★☆

Mr. Fillmore Goes to Washington ─────

Fillmore arrived in Washington, D.C., in December 1833, to take his seat in the House of Representatives. It was a time of great excitement. Andrew Jackson was serving his second term as president. Fillmore was part of the opposition to Jackson's Democrats. One opposition leader in the House was former president John Quincy Adams, who had been elected to the House after retiring from the presidency. In the Senate, a leader of the opposition was Henry Clay, the Kentuckian who had been a powerful legislator for nearly 20 years and had lost the presidential election to Jackson in 1832. Another was Daniel Webster of Massachusetts, known as the greatest orator in the Senate's history.

In the House, most positions were filled on the basis of *seniority* (how long a congressman had served), so first-term members had little power. Following tradition, Fillmore listened and learned. Outside the House, Senator Daniel Webster got to know Fillmore and introduced him to many leaders in Washington, including members of the Supreme Court.

Fillmore was appointed to the House committee that oversaw Washington, D.C. Just across the Potomac River from Virginia, Washington was a southern city where many residents owned slaves, and an active slave market allowed owners to buy or sell their human property. Fillmore expressed his

The Capitol building in Washington, D.C., about the time Fillmore arrived to serve in Congress. Later, as president, he would participate in plans to enlarge the building and replace the dome with the one we know today.

disapproval of the slave trade and urged that it be abolished in the nation's capital. He was also active in talks between the Anti-Masonic and National Republican parties, which aimed at creating a single party in opposition to the Democrats. By 1834, the new Whig party was established.

In 1834, Fillmore decided not to run for reelection to the House. Not all Anti-Masonic party members had joined the Whigs, and Fillmore said he did not feel comfortable running as a Whig in his home district. However, Fillmore soon grew restless back in Buffalo and longed to return to politics. So in 1836, he ran for Congress as a Whig and was elected. He would gain reelection in 1838 and 1840, serving until early in 1843.

In Congress Fillmore became a strong advocate of internal improvements such as bridges and roads. When the Democratic leadership voted on a rule to forbid debate on any petitions relating to slavery, Fillmore supported John Quincy Adams in opposing this so-called Gag Rule.

He supported the rights of the minority in the House in other circumstances as well. One day he was interrupted by the House Speaker when he was reading a report into the official record. In a stirring speech, he said, "The majority possesses all the power. The minority have nothing to protect them but the Constitution and the rules of the House; and if these are broken, then farewell to freedom, farewell to all that is dear to an American citizen!"

In 1840, in the midst of a severe national depression, the Whig candidates for office swept the elections, electing William Henry Harrison president, winning majorities in both the House and Senate, and electing twelve state governors. The Whigs gained the chairmanship of all committees in the House, and Fillmore was appointed chairman of the powerful House Committee on Ways and Means, which helped supervise the finances of the federal government.

Fillmore helped draft and pass important new tariff measures in 1842. *Tariffs*, which are taxes on goods imported from other countries, had long been an emotional issue between Whigs and Democrats. He also insisted on budgeting a grant of $30,000 for Samuel F. B. Morse, who was developing a seemingly magical system for sending messages across long distances almost instantly. It was called the telegraph.

The Call of Higher Office

Fillmore was becoming a national political figure. The *New York American* wrote that he was "dignified, cool, self-possessed, conciliating, clear, concise, and indefatigable," and that he showed "a majestic, high-toned eloquence, that astonished and even convinced." His pronouncements were usually moderate and carefully considered, making more friends than enemies.

A portrait of Millard Fillmore as he looked when serving in Congress.

By June 1842, Whigs were already thinking about the presidential elections in 1844. Tragically, William Henry Harrison had died after serving only one month as president. It was the first time a president had died in office, and Vice President John Tyler was sworn in as president. Unfortunately, Tyler proved to be very unpopular. He quarreled with Whigs in Congress and vetoed important Whig bills. He was finally thrown out of the Whig party altogether. The Whigs would need new candidates in 1844.

Whig newspapers in New York began suggesting that Millard Fillmore should be considered for vice president in 1844. Fillmore dismissed the suggestion as "a passing compliment by an unknown hand," but he may have been more interested than he let on. He declined to run again for Congress, and in early 1843 he returned to Buffalo and the "quiet enjoyment of my family and fireside." Still, it seemed that political plans were being made. That summer, former president John Quincy Adams visited Buffalo and praised Fillmore as a man of integrity and honor, urging him to return to public office.

Then Fillmore got caught in a tangled political web in New York State. The boss of the New York Whig party was his old friend and one-time supporter Thurlow Weed. However, Weed was supporting another New Yorker for vice president. Weed had helped elect William Seward as Whig governor of New York in 1838 and 1840, and now he wanted Seward to be nominated for vice president.

To get around Weed and Seward, Fillmore made an alliance with John Collier, a Whig who wanted the Whig nomination for governor in 1844. Fillmore would help Collier get nominated if Collier would support him for vice president. Seward heard about the alliance and announced he would not stand in Fillmore's way and would not run for vice president.

That might have ended the story, but Thurlow Weed was determined to keep his control of the party. Weed met with Fillmore and asked him to run for governor instead, breaking his deal with Collier. Fillmore refused.

That May, at the national Whig convention, Henry Clay, one of the party's founders, was nominated for president. Before a vice president could be nominated, Weed spread rumors among the delegates that if they nominated Seward, he would accept. Weed's tactics worked, but only partly. He made sure that Fillmore would not be considered, but Seward also lost the nomination when the delegates nominated Theodore Frelinghuysen of New Jersey.

With that fight over, Weed took charge of the nomination for governor. He convinced Collier to give up his own candidacy, then pleaded with Fillmore to run for governor for the good of the party. Fillmore was reluctant, but he finally agreed. He reasoned that even if he lost, his campaign would put him in a good position for national office in the future. "So I am in for it and there is no escape," he said.

Thurlow Weed, the boss of the New York Whig party. Weed supported Fillmore early in his career, but later the two men struggled for control of the New York Whigs.

Like most northern Whigs, Fillmore was opposed to the spread of slavery, and he was against *annexing* Texas, or making it part of U.S. territory. Then an independent republic, Texas had asked the United States to annex it. Northern Whigs were against annexation because Texas would almost certainly become a large new slave state. The party was divided over Texas, however. Southern Whigs were in favor of annexing Texas immediately. At the Baltimore convention, Henry Clay, the Whig candidate for president, had pledged that he would oppose the annexation of Texas. When southern Whigs protested, however, he seemed to change his mind, afraid that he would lose needed southern votes. He said that slavery should have nothing to do with annexing Texas, and that if it became part of the United States, it should do so "upon fair and just terms."

Clay's new position pleased no one, and it outraged the antislavery Whigs in New York. Some important Whig leaders stopped campaigning for him. Fillmore's race for governor suffered as support for Whig candidates began to melt away. It soon became clear that Clay would lose the presidential election, and that Fillmore would lose his first election ever. Fillmore was distraught, saying, "All is gone—but honor."

The defeat was a severe blow to Fillmore's political career. He returned to his law practice in Buffalo. In 1846, Whigs pleaded with Fillmore to run for governor again, but he refused. Then, in 1847, the position of state *comptroller* became vacant. Some said the position was as powerful as that of governor, since the comptroller was in charge of the state's finances. Fillmore ran and won by a landslide.

Excited to be back in government, Fillmore and Abigail moved to Albany. Their son Millard Powers was studying at Harvard University in Massachusetts, and their daughter Abby was attending a school in Lenox, Massachusetts, not far from Albany. Fillmore proved to be a very successful comptroller. He helped reorganize the state's finances and gained many friends in the state's Whig party. As he became a powerful member of the state government, Fillmore realized, as one historian has written, "henceforth his life was not to be passed in the quiet practice of law, but in the full blaze of public life where he was to be a prominent actor."

Chapter 4

A War with Mexico ——————————

In 1844, Democrat James K. Polk defeated Whig Henry Clay for the presidency partly on his pledge to annex Texas as part of the United States. Even before he took office in March 1845, Congress voted for annexation. By December that year, Texas was admitted to the Union as a state. Polk's supporters cheered his actions, but the reaction in Mexico was very different. The Mexican government threatened to go to war. It had never given up its claim to all of Texas, and it had long disputed the proper border between Mexico and land the Texans claimed.

President Polk decided to test the Mexican government. In early 1846, he ordered the army, commanded by Zachary Taylor, to march into the disputed territory and to build a fort on the river called the Rio Grande. Mexican troops gathered across the river. In April, they crossed the Rio Grande and ambushed a U.S. scouting party there. When President Polk got the news, he asked Congress for a declaration of war against Mexico for crossing into land claimed by Texas and attacking an American force. Congress declared war on May 13.

In the meantime, General Taylor and his army had won the first two victories of the war and soon drove the Mexican troops back across the Rio Grande. That fall, Taylor's men crossed the Rio Grande and captured Monterrey, the most important settlement in that part of Mexico. Early in 1847, a Mexican army attacked Taylor's force at Buena Vista, near Monterrey. Even though the Mexicans far outnumbered his army, Taylor won his most famous victory. In two days of desperate fighting, his army managed to hold its ground. The Mexicans suffered heavy losses and were forced to retreat. His success in battle made Taylor a national hero and a leading prospect for the Whig nomination for president in 1848.

After Buena Vista, a U.S. force sailed to Veracruz, on Mexico's Caribbean coast. It captured that city, then marched inland toward Mexico City, the country's capital. In September 1847, Mexico City surrendered. Mexico was forced to *cede*, or give up, nearly 500,000 square miles (1.3 million km^2) of its territory to the United States in return for $15 million and other U.S. concessions.

At Buena Vista in 1847, General Zachary Taylor defeated a Mexican army much larger than his own and became a national hero. Less than two years later, he was elected President of the United States.

Suddenly the United States included all or most of present-day California, Nevada, Arizona, Utah, and New Mexico, and parts of five other states. President Polk's administration had also negotiated a treaty with Great Britain which gave the United States possession of the Oregon region south of the 49th parallel—the present-day states of Washington, Oregon, and Idaho, and parts of Montana and Wyoming. These huge new territories set the scene for the political battles for the next four years.

Presidential Politics

As the 1848 presidential election approached, the one great question was whether the new territories should allow or prohibit slavery. Both the Democrats and the Whigs were divided on the issue. Southerners of both parties rejoiced that Texas was already a slave state, and they believed that slavery should be allowed in the new territories as well. Northerners, many of whom had opposed the war with Mexico, were determined that the spread of slavery should be stopped.

In the Democratic party, President Polk had pledged to serve only one term as president, and he refused to run for reelection. At the national convention, the Democrats nominated Michigan senator Lewis Cass. He was a northerner, but he appealed to southern Democrats as well, since he believed that the people who lived in the territories should decide the issue of slavery for themselves.

The Whigs believed they had a winner in General Zachary Taylor. He had won glorious victories in the U.S.-Mexican War, giving him appeal to patriotic Americans in all regions. Because he had never held an elective office or spoken widely about political affairs, he had few political enemies. Finally, he appealed to southern Whigs because he now lived in Louisiana, where he owned cotton plantations and slaves.

Northern Whigs who opposed slavery were disappointed by the nomination. "The free states will not submit!" they shouted, fearing that Taylor was "soft" on the slavery issue. To keep the party together, they demanded a vice-presidential candidate from the North.

Taylor's own preference to run for vice president was Abbott Lawrence, a Massachusetts merchant and congressman. However, Lawrence owned a cloth-making business which bought large quantities of cotton from southern plantations. Northerners complained that if Lawrence was nominated, there would be "cotton on both ends of the ticket." As a compromise, John Collier of New York nominated a "surprise" candidate, New Yorker Millard Fillmore. The convention approved and Fillmore accepted the nomination.

Fillmore and Taylor had never met. In background and personal appearance, they were an odd match. Taylor had been born into a prominent family and had become both a prosperous plantation owner and a military hero. Yet he dressed carelessly, and his weather-beaten face made him look like a frontiersman. In the army, his nickname was "Old Rough-and-Ready." Fillmore had been born in poverty and had struggled to gain a secure place as a lawyer and politician. Yet he was tall and handsome, and dressed elegantly. Taylor knew little about the workings of the federal government. For example, he mistakenly believed that the vice president was a member of the president's cabinet. Fillmore had served in Washington and knew from firsthand experience how the government worked.

After the convention, Fillmore wrote a note to Taylor. He said he was pleased to be with Taylor and hoped they'd soon meet. In his response, Taylor assured Fillmore that he felt that the vice presidential nominee would be "generally acceptable to the Whigs of the South," and "prove a tower of strength in the North." It seemed that things were off to a good start.

Election

Even though the slavery question was the big issue of the day, both Whigs and Democrats avoided it during the campaign. With their own parties split on the issue, they felt they could bring it up only indirectly. They emphasized the need to find a way to keep the United States together, or in the terms of the day, to preserve the Union. Fillmore condemned extremists on both sides of the slavery issue. He spoke of "putting an end to all ideas of disunion," and leaving "the fanatics and disunionists, north and south, without the hope of destroying the fair fabric of our constitution."

Like the other candidates, Fillmore had expressed views on slavery that could be interpreted in different ways. Northerners were confident that he considered slavery an evil. Southerners noted that he seemed willing to let slavery exist, since he believed that states and territories had the right to choose it for themselves. Regardless of his own feelings about slavery, Fillmore later wrote, "The

A colorful banner for Taylor and Fillmore designed for the presidential campaign of 1848.

Senator Henry Clay (above) first entered Congress in 1811, when Fillmore was still a boy. Later, he was a founding member of the Whig Party and twice a candidate for president. In 1850, he created a plan for a compromise between North and South and presented it to the Senate (right) in a speech that lasted five hours.

fashion the Missouri Compromise. It set a pattern of admitting an equal number of free and slave states to the Union, and it forbade slavery in most of the territories of the Louisiana Purchase. Now, Clay believed, another wide-reaching compromise was necessary to keep the country from breaking apart.

In December 1849, President Taylor presented his plan for the admission of California and New Mexico as free states. Clay ignored the president's plan, and early in 1850, he outlined his own compromise plan in a five-hour speech in the Senate. It was a huge proposal that sought to deal with many pressing issues. Some of his proposals pleased those who were against extending slavery, and others pleased those who were in favor.

For antislavery congressmen, Clay proposed that California should be admitted as a state with its antislavery constitution and that the slave trade in Washington, D.C., be ended. He proposed that other new territories be organized without deciding the slavery issue, leaving it to the will of the territories' residents. For proslavery congressmen, he proposed a greatly strengthened law on the return of fugitive (runaway) slaves, forcing northern states to catch former slaves and return them to their owners in the South.

Taylor remained silent, refusing to support Clay's broader compromise and insisting that the Congress act on parts of his own plan. Debate in Congress became more and more emotional. Daniel Webster of Massachusetts, known to be a strong opponent of slavery, spoke eloquently to the Senate, urging that senators set their differences aside and agree to Clay's compromise to save the Union. Others, however, were in no mood to compromise. John C. Calhoun of South Carolina said that Clay's plan did not satisfy the South and warned that southern states might *secede* (leave the United States) rather than give up their constitutional rights. Senator Seward of New York denounced the proposed fugitive slave law as a "pact with the devil."

Clay put all the provisions of the compromise together in one "omnibus" bill, forcing Congress to vote on the whole program, rather than on its individual pieces. He criticized President Taylor's plan. Taylor still refused to agree to the compromise.

As vice president, Fillmore presided over the debates in the Senate. He took a strong stand on preserving order. On April 3, 1850, he announced that he would demand that any senator who "violated the decorum of the debate," return to his seat. "A slight attack, or even insinuation of a personal character, often provokes a more severe retort, which brings out a more disorderly reply, each Senator feeling a justification in the previous aggression. There is, therefore, no point so proper to interpose for the preservation of order as to check the first violation of it."

Two weeks later, a fierce argument erupted between Henry Foote of Mississippi and Thomas Hart Benton of Missouri. At one point, Benton stood up and walked toward Foote. The Mississippian took a pistol from his pocket and aimed it at Benton.

"I have no pistols! Let him fire," shouted Benton dramatically. "Stand out of the way, and let the assassin fire!"

Senator Daniel Webster (above) urged the Senate to pass Clay's compromise to save the Union. John
C. Calhoun (right) sternly opposed the compromise because he believed it was not fair to the South.

Brady.   N. Y.

Other senators separated Foote and Benton, and no one was hurt. Fillmore watched in utter shock. The insults, name-calling, and ugly incidents saddened Fillmore. As vice president he could only control the debate. He could not speak on the issues or vote unless the Senate was tied. He was also discouraged that he had no influence with President Taylor.

Then on the Fourth of July, President Taylor got sick. Five days later, he died. Now, at a critical moment in the country's history, Millard Fillmore was sworn in as president. His life would never be the same.

Chapter 5

Growth and Change

When Millard Fillmore entered the White House in 1850 as the 13th president, the United States was a very different place than it had been in 1800, the year of his birth.

In 1800, there were only 5 million people in 16 states, about half in the North and half in the South. Nearly all of them lived between the Atlantic coast and the Appalachian Mountains. By 1850, the country had 23 million people in 30 states (California would become the 31st state later that year). The northern states had 14 million people and the southern states only 9 million, and the North was growing at a faster pace. Most amazing, in 1850, 10 million people lived west of the Appalachian Mountains, compared with 13 million along the Eastern Seaboard. Ohio and Tennessee were among the five most populous states in the Union.

The States During the Presidency of Millard Fillmore

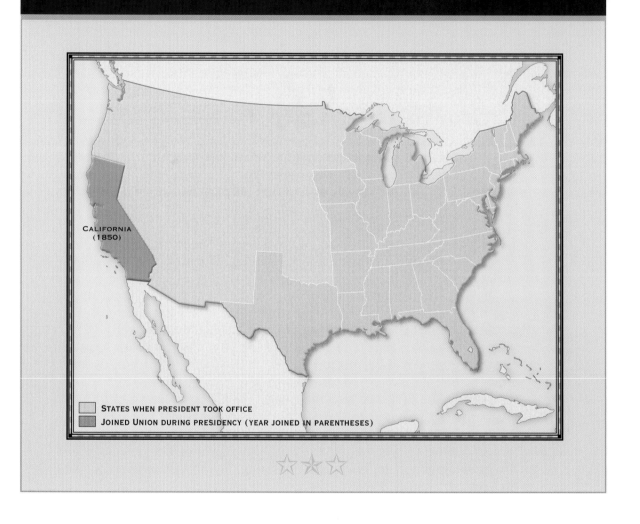

CALIFORNIA
(1850)

STATES WHEN PRESIDENT TOOK OFFICE
JOINED UNION DURING PRESIDENCY (YEAR JOINED IN PARENTHESES)

The northeastern states had become the center for manufacturing and international trade. The north central states were becoming the nation's breadbasket, producing most of its grain. The southern states produced food crops, but they also grew about 80 percent of the cotton in the world.

Now the country had to plan for the gigantic new territories west of the Mississippi River. Arkansas, Missouri, and Iowa were among the fastest growing states, and tens of thousands were heading for California, where gold had been discovered. With such rapid growth and change, there were many tensions between regions of the country. Westerners resented the wealth and power of eastern bankers and merchants. Easterners made fun of the crude settlers on the western frontier.

The biggest dispute, however, was between the North and the South. As the North grew at a faster rate, it outnumbered the South by more people each year. At the same time, more and more northerners began to believe that the enslavement of African Americans was wrong. Southerners began to fear for their way of life. If northern antislavery leaders gained control of Congress and the federal government, would they restrict slavery or even outlaw it altogether? How would the South's agricultural economy survive without the millions of slaves to plant and harvest its crops?

Millard Fillmore inherited these pressures when he was sworn in as president. Through his political career, he had worked toward finding compromises that would help regions work together and strengthen the nation. Even though he personally disliked slavery, he believed that the Constitution allowed it. He said that he would base his policies on the Constitution.

The Compromise of 1850

Fillmore was a strong supporter of the compromise proposed by Henry Clay. Only days before President Taylor's fatal illness, Fillmore had told the president that if a Senate vote on the compromise was tied, as vice president he would cast the tie-breaking vote in favor of it, even against the president's wishes. With two senators each from 15 free states and 15 slave states, a tie was a real possibility.

Now that he was president, Fillmore no longer presided over the Senate and would not be able to cast a tie-breaking vote. He soon made it clear, however, that he would use his power and influence as president to get the compromise passed. "God knows that I detest slavery," Fillmore wrote to Daniel Webster later that year, "but it is an existing evil, for which we are not responsible, and we must endure it, and give it such protection as is guaranteed by the constitution, till we can get rid of it without destroying the last hope of free government in the world."

At the end of July, the omnibus bill including all elements of Clay's compromise was voted down. Supporters of the bill were discouraged, and Henry Clay, aged and ill, left Washington for a rest. At this point, the campaign for the compromise found a new leader. A first-term senator, Democrat Stephen Douglas of Illinois, became its strongest sponsor. With Fillmore's support, Douglas proposed breaking the compromise apart and passing the provisions one at a time. As the summer wore on, five different bills were debated and passed by the House and the Senate, reflecting all the main points of Clay's plan. Fillmore signed the bills in September, making the Compromise of 1850 the law of the land.

"The long agony is over," Fillmore wrote soon afterward in a letter to New York's Senator Hamilton Fish. He knew there were still dangers ahead, but, he wrote, "I am rejoiced" and expressed his belief that the compromise would "restore harmony and peace in our distracted country." A celebration of the signing featured the Marine Band and the firing of a 100-gun salute.

The celebrations soon ended, however, as people North and South began to see how the compromise would affect them. Far from restoring harmony and peace, it soon pushed the country and the Fillmore presidency into a swirl of controversy that increased tensions in the country and ended Fillmore's political career.

Many in the North had had little contact with slavery. The Fugitive Slave Act caused them to focus on it and to realize what the life of a slave must be like. Secret networks sprang up through the northern states to provide safe passage for escaping slaves from the South to Canada, where the Fugitive Slave Act could not reach them. This network came to be known as the *Underground Railroad*. Vermont and other states in the North passed laws that protected the rights of accused fugitives. Some members of Congress even called on citizens to defy the Fugitive Slave Act openly.

Fillmore, for his part, remained committed to the whole compromise, including the Fugitive Slave Act. He promised to uphold the law, even if he had to send in federal troops to do so. In one case, a southern slaveholder tracked down a slave who had run away. When the slaveholder tried to take the runaway into custody, the runaway and his friends killed him. Fillmore asked the courts to charge the killers with treason, but the courts rejected his request.

Perhaps the most lasting effect of the Fugitive Slave Act was a book, written soon after its passage and published in 1852. *Uncle Tom's Cabin*, by Harriet Beecher Stowe, was a novel that portrayed the life of a group of slaves during the period. Hundreds of thousands read it, and it greatly strengthened the outcry against slavery and the Fugitive Slave Act.

Harriet Beecher Stowe was the daughter of a famous New England preacher. From 1832 to 1850 she lived with her husband in Cincinnati, Ohio, where she gained a deep sympathy for the slaves who lived just across the Ohio River in the slave state of Kentucky. Shortly after moving back to New England in 1850, she wrote *Uncle Tom's Cabin*. It appeared first as a serial in an antislavery magazine and came out as a book in 1852. In its first year, it sold 300,000 copies.

In the book, a slaveowner falls into debt and must sell two of his slaves, an old man named Uncle Tom, and a bright young boy named Harry. Harry's mother, Eliza, and her husband make daring escapes across the Ohio River and are carried by the Underground Railroad to Canada. Tom is carried down the Ohio and Mississippi Rivers to be sold. There he falls into the hands of the cruel slaveowner Simon Legree.

An early poster advertising *Uncle Tom's Cabin*, a novel that dramatized the sufferings of slaves and became a huge best-seller in the northern states.

Stowe portrayed the physical and mental abuse suffered by slaves, and created characters, such as Tom, Eliza, and George Harris, to whom average readers could relate. It brought the evils of slavery to life for thousands of Americans and may have convinced many of them that slavery should be abolished. According to legend, when President Abraham Lincoln met Harriet Beecher Stowe during the Civil War, he said, "So you're the little woman who wrote the book that started this Great War!"

Progress and Prosperity

Even though the Compromise of 1850 overshadowed much of Fillmore's presidency, it was not the only thing that attracted the president's attention. In spite of the bitter arguments over slavery, the country was going through a period of great prosperity and progress.

In 1851, the New York and Erie Railway was completed, connecting New York City to the Great Lakes, greatly reducing the time required for travel or shipping from the Great Lakes to the Atlantic Ocean. Fillmore and other dignitaries traveled the route in a ceremonial train to celebrate the great event. Dressed in his best finery, including a frock coat, top hat, and ascot tie, Fillmore greeted the crowds along the way by appearing at the rear of the train. His secretary of state, the elderly Daniel Webster, sat in a rocking chair secured to the open flatcar, so that he could see in all directions.

Later, Fillmore attended the openings of other railroad systems in the United States and Canada. He also celebrated the opening of regular steamship service from New England to Liverpool, England. Thousands came to Newport, Rhode Island, to see the first ship off and were treated to a magnificent fireworks display.

As roads around major cities improved, wealthy people commissioned the design of luxurious horse-drawn coaches. A group of New York Whigs made

The New York & Erie Railroad connected New York City, on the Atlantic Ocean, to Buffalo, on Lake Erie. As a resident of Buffalo, Millard Fillmore was proud to celebrate the completion of this important new line.

a gift of such a coach to Abigail Fillmore for her use in Washington. In a letter to Fillmore describing the gift, the donor wrote, "It is of the richest materials, and finished in a style that reflects credit on the artisan employed to do the work. The body and the running gear are painted dark invisible green, and the door panels are relieved by a very . . . artistical painting representing the coat and arms of New York. . . . On each side of the driver's box is a silver lamp, very ornamental and chaste. A spread eagle of solid silver surmounts each of the reflectors, and the plated glass . . . is fitted in diamond-shape, and thus presents a neat and rich appearance. . . . The seats . . . are covered in rich blue watered silk, through which a vine or sprig of white run, that in a glare of light resembles burnished silver. They are stuffed with curled hair of the best quality. [There is a] rich Turkey carpet on the bottom of the carriage. . . . To each of . . . [the ten windows] is attached a spring curtain of beautiful blue silk finished with rich festoons and tassels."

After the passage of the Compromise of 1850, Fillmore was sometimes lonely, having few friends and few supporters. He complained that northern critics considered him a supporter of slavery and southern critics thought he was an abolitionist. "I am neither," he said. Life in the White House could be lonely as well. Abigail was often ill, and left official entertaining to others.

Abigail's love of books and reading continued, however. When she moved into the White House, she was surprised that there was no permanent White House library. At her request, Congress appropriated funds for a library, and she spent many hours choosing appropriate volumes for the enjoyment of her family and later presidential families. She also enjoyed inviting great writers to the White House. During her time there she entertained Washington Irving, author of "The Legend of Sleepy Hollow" and many other stories, novels, and histories.

Abigail Fillmore was Millard Fillmore's most important supporter and friend from his teen years through his presidency. She had been his most influential teacher and encouraged him to improve his skills. After their marriage, she defied custom by continuing to work as a teacher outside their home. She was an avid reader and collector of books, and an amateur musician, playing the piano and the harp.

When her husband was in Congress, Abigail often watched the proceedings from the ladies' gallery and later discussed the day's events with him. In 1842, she suffered a bad fall and severely injured her ankle, which made it painful for her to stand, and she suffered from other illnesses. When Fillmore was elected vice

Abigail Fillmore, who first met Millard Fillmore when he was her student, played an important role in his rise from poverty to the White House.

president, she remained in Buffalo much of the time. When he became president, she returned to Washington and served as hostess at regular weekly White House receptions and dinners. The Fillmores' pretty and engaging daughter, Abby, often served as hostess when Abigail was ill. The Fillmores carried on a quiet family life in the White House, enjoying music, reading, and conversation.

Abigail opposed slavery, and according to legend, she urged her husband to veto the Fugitive Slave Act. It is said that she considered it an immoral law and that she feared it would end her husband's career in politics. Sadly, she died only a few weeks after Fillmore's term as president ended.

She also met two of her favorite British authors, the novelists Charles Dickens and William Makepeace Thackeray.

Other Accomplishments

In foreign affairs, Fillmore set in motion an American expedition to Japan. For 200 years, Japanese military leaders had kept their country closed to the outside world, allowing only one Dutch ship to visit once a year. Fillmore believed that Japan might someday be an important trading partner. American merchants pointed out that they needed a port in eastern Asia where they could buy coal and other provisions.

Fillmore commissioned Commodore Matthew Perry to lead an expedition to persuade the Japanese that trade with America was in their best interest. Perry left Norfolk, Virginia, in November 1852, with two years' worth of provisions, two telegraph transmitters, and an interpreter. Eight months later, on July 14, 1853, four months after Fillmore's presidency ended, he reached Japan.

Perry went ashore at the small village of Kurihama. The Japanese gave the Americans a tense greeting, sending 5,000 well-armed Japanese soldiers to meet them. Perry presented his papers, including a letter from Fillmore to the emperor of Japan, which requested protection for shipwrecked American seamen, the right

A Japanese woodblock print shows one of Commodore Perry's huge "black ships" arriving in Japan. The Japanese had never seen a steam-powered ship and were terrified by the billowing black smoke that poured out of its smokestacks.

to buy coal, and the opening of one or more Japanese ports to trade. The Japanese were reluctant, but they did agree to another visit. On the second expedition, Perry succeeded in negotiating a trade agreement. Fillmore's support of Perry's initial trip laid the groundwork for his later success.

Fillmore could also claim accomplishments in other areas. He succeeded in reducing postal rates (which resulted in greatly expanded use of the postal service). He encouraged the establishment of a home for poor veterans. He also persuaded Congress to appropriate funds to improve conditions in Washington, D.C., arranging for adequate water supply and the construction of new bridges over the Potomac River.

During the height of the debate on the great compromise, Fillmore even had a chance to influence the design of the Capitol building. In September 1850, he concluded that none of the proposed plans for enlarging the building was satisfactory. He appointed Thomas U. Walter as Architect of the Capitol. Together,

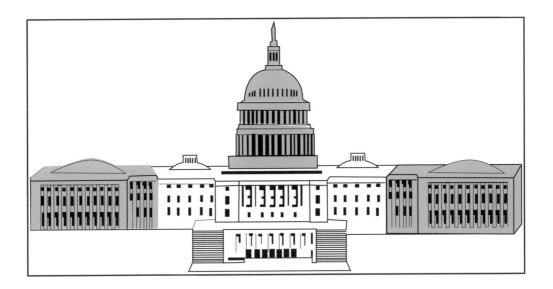

Fillmore appointed Thomas U. Walter as Architect of the Capitol. Walter designed large new wings on both sides of the building and a majestic new dome. Work began during Fillmore's presidency and took more than ten years to complete.

they combined ideas from several of those plans so that the expansion would not, as Fillmore said, "mar the harmony and beauty of the present structure."

The Election of 1852

Fillmore was reluctant to run for a full term as president in 1852. It was clear that continuing anger over the Compromise of 1850 had reduced his popularity, and he knew as well as anyone how stormy the next four years might be. The Whig party itself was in a shambles, on the verge of dividing into proslavery and anti-slavery splinters. Still, party leaders urged him to put his name up for the nomination, and he reluctantly agreed.

The Whig national convention met in Baltimore, Maryland, in June 1852. At the end of the first ballot, Fillmore had the most votes, but on later ballots his support declined. Finally, after 53 ballots, the convention nominated another hero of the U.S.-Mexican War, General Winfield Scott. It turned out that Scott was a dreadful campaigner, and he lost the election to Democrat Franklin Pierce. Scott was the last nominee of a united Whig party. Before the next presidential election, the party had splintered. It would never elect another president.

As his time in office came to a close, Fillmore was satisfied that he had done the best job he was capable of under the most difficult circumstances. In his

last address to Congress, he said, "I claim only to have discharged [my duties] to the best of my humble ability with a single eye to the public good, and it is with devout gratitude in retiring from office that I leave the country in a state of peace and prosperity."

Chapter 6

After the White House

Tragedies

President-elect Pierce's inauguration day, March 4, 1853, was snowy, cold, and blustery. Both Millard and Abigail Fillmore attended, standing out in the cold, wet weather for hours. Abigail, never in the best of health, was feeling chilled and faint. "She was braving it all with a weak smile," one historian wrote, "but her face was drawn, her lips pinched and blue, her feet moving in the slush and water to keep warm."

By the next day she had a bad cold, and she couldn't seem to shake off its effects. Later in March, she got pneumonia and began to run a high fever. Millard and their son and daughter comforted Abigail at her bedside. The best physicians in Washington were called, but there was little they could do. On March 30, 1853, Abigail Fillmore died.

Fillmore was 53 when his term ended, the youngest retired president in history. He and Abigail had planned to travel widely and then return to Buffalo to build a new house. After Abigail's death, Fillmore was grief stricken. "I feel I have no strength, no resolution, no energy," he wrote several weeks later. "The prospect is gloomy."

He canceled plans for the new house and cast around for something to do. At first he thought he might return to his law practice, but no president had ever returned to the private practice of law, and so he decided against it. He returned to Buffalo and at first lived a quiet life of reading and writing, comforted by the company of his daughter Abby.

Fillmore turned once again to politics. He arranged a tour of the southern and border states with Nathan K. Hall, his former law partner, and John P. Kennedy, who had served in his administration as secretary of the navy. The trio "attracted much attention," wrote the *Ohio State Journal* on March 12, 1854, "both from their high positions among the leading men of the nation and the fact that they ranked among the best-looking men of the country."

Later that year, tragedy struck once again. In July 1854, Fillmore's daughter Abby visited a family outside Buffalo. There she caught the deadly disease cholera and died in a few days. She was only 22. Once again, Fillmore went into mourning.

Mary Abigail (Abby) Fillmore, Fillmore's only daughter, died at the age of 22 in 1854, only a year after her mother's death.

One More Campaign

Meanwhile, the old Whig party had divided, and new parties were seeking attention. One was the American party, to which many northern Whigs were attracted. It favored many old Whig policies, but it gained the most attention for a new issue. The party was upset about the growing influence of recent immigrants in politics and public life. In New York and other large cities, immigrants from Ireland were organizing political clubs and establishing Roman Catholic schools to educate their children. Political revolutionaries driven out of Germany in 1848 were introducing radical ideas from Europe. The American party supported new laws that would allow only men born in the United States to hold political offices. It also wanted to revise the law to require immigrants to live in the United States for 21 years (rather than 5 years) before applying for citizenship and gaining the right to vote.

American party members became better known as "Know-Nothings." The party secretly supported candidates from other parties, instructing its members how to vote. If questioned about the party's operation, members were told to say, "I know nothing." Outsiders were amused by this secrecy, and soon the party was widely known as the Know-Nothing party. Advertisers even named products for it, including Know-Nothing Tea and Know-Nothing toothpicks.

Fillmore expressed interest in the party and its platform. In early 1855, he wrote in a letter to a friend that he agreed with the Know-Nothings that only those "reared in a free country" should be allowed to run for office in the United States. He expressed some interest in running under the party's banner in a future political race.

In the meantime, he planned a long overseas tour. He sailed for Europe on the steamship *Atlantic* early in 1855, creating a stir wherever he went. He visited England, Ireland, France, Italy, Egypt, Prussia (a part of present-day Germany), Palestine, and Turkey. "It is better to wear out than rust out," he wrote to a friend, "and as my political life has unfortunately deprived me of my profession, perhaps I can do nothing better than to diversify my pursuits by traveling."

In London he shared a visitors' box overlooking the British House of Commons with former president Martin Van Buren. At the opera, he sat with members of the royal family in their private box. When he was presented to Queen Victoria, she remarked that he was the most handsome man she'd ever encountered. In France he met Emperor Napoléon III. In Rome, to the surprise of anti-Catholics in the Know-Nothing party back home, he had an audience with the pope.

At Oxford University in England, Fillmore was offered an honorary degree written by long tradition in Latin. Fillmore gracefully turned it down, saying, "I had

Fillmore married Caroline McIntosh, a widow, in 1858. They bought a fine mansion in Buffalo, where they lived until Fillmore's death in 1874.

Although Fillmore was widely respected during his retirement in Buffalo, he was still remembered as the president who signed the hated Fugitive Slave Act. In 1865, the night after Abraham Lincoln was shot and killed by a Confederate sympathizer, hecklers gathered outside his house and vandals blackened its walls.

Fillmore continued to maintain a quiet interest in public affairs. In 1874, he suffered a series of strokes. On March 8, with his wife at his bedside, he died.

Fillmore's Legacy

At the time of Fillmore's death, the *New York Times* recalled that Fillmore had left the presidency with "the country at peace with all the world and enjoying a high degree of prosperity." Since then he has not been seen kindly by history. After the Union won the Civil War and slavery was abolished, historians looked back at the Compromise of 1850 as a betrayal of morality which protected slavery rather than ending it. They saw Fillmore, who worked so hard for its passage, as a man who had worked for an evil cause. Fillmore's reputation was also damaged by his association with the Know-Nothings, a group that preached intolerance of immigrants and of Roman Catholicism.

Some recent historians have been kinder to Fillmore. They point out that the Compromise of 1850 was an intelligent effort to build a bridge between increasingly divided regions. It did not succeed in ending the division, but it did

Fillmore was active in many good causes in Buffalo and was the city's most distinguished resident. After his death, the city honored him by erecting this larger-than-life statue.

postpone the horrors of a civil war. If Fillmore had supported outlawing slavery in the new territories, they say, it is likely southern states would have seceded sooner, bringing on a civil war.

Whatever his failures, Fillmore was a decent, upstanding man who tried to do what he thought was right, despite the consequences. He was not wise enough or persuasive enough to end the divisions of the country, but he did all he was able to do.

"The man who can look upon a crisis without being willing to offer himself upon the altar of his country is not fit for public trust," Fillmore once said. Fillmore did not succeed, but he was brave enough to take up the challenge.

Fast Facts · Millard Fillmore

Birth:	January 7, 1800
Birthplace:	Locke Township, New York
Parents:	Nathaniel Fillmore and Phoebe Millard Fillmore
Brothers & Sisters:	Olive Armstrong (b. 1797)
	Cyrus (b. 1804?)
	Almon Hopkins (b. 1806)
	Calvin Turner (b. 1810)
	Julia (b. 1812)
	Darius Ingraham (b. 1814)
	Charles Dewitt (b. 1817)
	Phoebe Maria (b. 1819)
Education:	Largely self-taught
Occupation:	Lawyer
Marriage:	To Abigail Powers Fillmore (1798–1853), February 5, 1826
	To Caroline McIntosh (1813–1881), February 16, 1858
Children:	(see First Lady Fast Facts at right)
Political Parties:	Anti-Masonic, National Republican, Whig, American
Public Offices:	1828–1831 Member, New York State Assembly
	1833–1835 Member, U.S. House of Representatives
	1837–1843 Member, U.S. House of Representatives
	1847 New York State Comptroller
	1849–1850 Vice President of the U.S.
	1850–1853 Thirteenth President of the United States
His Vice President:	(None)
Major Actions as President:	1850 Appointed Daniel Webster Secretary of State
	1850 Supported and signed the Compromise of 1850
	1852 Reduced postage rates from 5 cents to 3 cents
	1852 Authorized mission of Commodore Perry to Japan (1852)
Death:	March 8, 1874
Age at Death:	74 years
Burial Place:	Forest Lawn Cemetery, Buffalo, New York

Fast Facts Abigail Powers Fillmore

Born:	March 13, 1798
Birthplace:	Stillwater, New York
Parents:	Lemuel and Abigail Newland Powers
Education:	Taught at home
Marriage:	To Millard Fillmore, February 5, 1826
Children:	Millard Powers Fillmore (1828–1889)
	Mary Abigail (Abby) Fillmore (1832–1854)
Death:	March 30, 1853 at Washington, D.C.
Age at Death:	55 years
Burial Place:	Forest Lawn Cemetery, Buffalo, New York

Timeline

1800	1823	1826	1828	1830
Millard Fillmore is born January 7, in Locke Township, New York.	Opens law practice in East Aurora, New York.	Marries Abigail Powers, February 5.	Son, Millard Powers, is born; Fillmore is elected to the New York State Assembly.	Family moves to Buffalo, New York.

1847	1848	1848	1849	1850
Elected comptroller of New York State.	Gains Whig nomination for vice president, July.	Zachary Taylor and Fillmore elected president and vice president, November.	Taylor and Fillmore take office, March.	Henry Clay presents compromise proposal January; Fillmore presides over historic Senate debates.

1854	1855	1856	1858	1874
Daughter Abby dies at age 22.	Begins world tour; meets Queen Victoria, Napoléon III, Pope Pius IX.	Nominated as American party candidate for president, runs a poor third.	Marries Caroline McIntosh.	Dies March 8 in Buffalo, New York.

1832

Daughter, Mary Abigail (Abby), is born; Fillmore is elected to U.S. House of Representatives, serves 1833–1835.

1836

Elected to second term in House and later reelected twice; serves 1837–1843.

1841

Appointed chairman of House Ways and Means Committee.

1844

Seeks but loses Whig nomination for vice president; runs for governor of New York and loses.

1846

U.S.-Mexican War begins.

1850

Zachary Taylor dies July 9, Fillmore sworn in as president.

1850

Fillmore signs bills making up the Compromise of 1850, September.

1852

Authorizes mission of Commodore Perry to Japan.

1852

Loses Whig nomination for president.

1853

Leaves office March 3; Abigail Fillmore dies March 30.

Table of Presidents

	1. George Washington	**2. John Adams**	**3. Thomas Jefferson**	**4. James Madison**
Took office	Apr 30 1789	Mar 4 1797	Mar 4 1801	Mar 4 1809
Left office	Mar 3 1797	Mar 3 1801	Mar 3 1809	Mar 3 1817
Birthplace	Westmoreland Co, VA	Braintree, MA	Shadwell, VA	Port Conway, VA
Birth date	Feb 22 1732	Oct 20 1735	Apr 13 1743	Mar 16 1751
Death date	Dec 14 1799	July 4 1826	July 4 1826	June 28 1836

	9. William H. Harrison	**10. John Tyler**	**11. James K. Polk**	**12. Zachary Taylor**
Took office	Mar 4 1841	Apr 6 1841	Mar 4 1845	Mar 5 1849
Left office	Apr 4 1841•	Mar 3 1845	Mar 3 1849	July 9 1850•
Birthplace	Berkeley, VA	Greenway, VA	Mecklenburg Co, NC	Barboursville, VA
Birth date	Feb 9 1773	Mar 29 1790	Nov 2 1795	Nov 24 1784
Death date	Apr 4 1841	Jan 18 1862	June 15 1849	July 9 1850

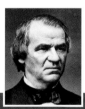   

	17. Andrew Johnson	**18. Ulysses S. Grant**	**19. Rutherford B. Hayes**	**20. James A. Garfield**
Took office	Apr 15 1865	Mar 4 1869	Mar 4 1877	Mar 4 1881
Left office	Mar 3 1869	Mar 3 1877	Mar 3 1881	Sept 19 1881•
Birthplace	Raleigh, NC	Point Pleasant, OH	Delaware, OH	Orange, OH
Birth date	Dec 29 1808	Apr 27 1822	Oct 4 1822	Nov 19 1831
Death date	July 31 1875	July 23 1885	Jan 17 1893	Sept 19 1881

5. James Monroe

Mar 4 1817

Mar 3 1825

Westmoreland Co, VA

Apr 28 1758

July 4 1831

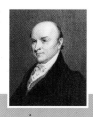

6. John Quincy Adams

Mar 4 1825

Mar 3 1829

Braintree, MA

July 11 1767

Feb 23 1848

7. Andrew Jackson

Mar 4 1829

Mar 3 1837

The Waxhaws, SC

Mar 15 1767

June 8 1845

8. Martin Van Buren

Mar 4 1837

Mar 3 1841

Kinderhook, NY

Dec 5 1782

July 24 1862

13. Millard Fillmore

July 9 1850

Mar 3 1853

Locke Township, NY

Jan 7 1800

Mar 8 1874

14. Franklin Pierce

Mar 4 1853

Mar 3 1857

Hillsborough, NH

Nov 23 1804

Oct 8 1869

15. James Buchanan

Mar 4 1857

Mar 3 1861

Cove Gap, PA

Apr 23 1791

June 1 1868

16. Abraham Lincoln

Mar 4 1861

Apr 15 1865•

Hardin Co, KY

Feb 12 1809

Apr 15 1865

21. Chester A. Arthur

Sept 19 1881

Mar 3 1885

Fairfield, VT

Oct 5 1830

Nov 18 1886

22. Grover Cleveland

Mar 4 1885

Mar 3 1889

Caldwell, NJ

Mar 18 1837

June 24 1908

23. Benjamin Harrison

Mar 4 1889

Mar 3 1893

North Bend, OH

Aug 20 1833

Mar 13 1901

24. Grover Cleveland

Mar 4 1893

Mar 3 1897

Caldwell, NJ

Mar 18 1837

June 24 1908

25. William McKinley | **26. Theodore Roosevelt** | **27. William H. Taft** | **28. Woodrow Wilson**

Took office	Mar 4 1897	Sept 14 1901	Mar 4 1909	Mar 4 1913
Left office	**Sept 14 1901•**	Mar 3 1909	Mar 3 1913	Mar 3 1921
Birthplace	Niles, OH	New York, NY	Cincinnati, OH	Staunton, VA
Birth date	Jan 29 1843	Oct 27 1858	Sept 15 1857	Dec 28 1856
Death date	Sept 14 1901	Jan 6 1919	Mar 8 1930	Feb 3 1924

33. Harry S. Truman | **34. Dwight D. Eisenhower** | **35. John F. Kennedy** | **36. Lyndon B. Johnson**

Took office	Apr 12 1945	Jan 20 1953	Jan 20 1961	Nov 22 1963
Left office	Jan 20 1953	Jan 20 1961	**Nov 22 1963•**	Jan 20 1969
Birthplace	Lamar, MO	Denison, TX	Brookline, MA	Johnson City, TX
Birth date	May 8 1884	Oct 14 1890	May 29 1917	Aug 27 1908
Death date	Dec 26 1972	Mar 28 1969	Nov 22 1963	Jan 22 1973

41. George Bush | **42. Bill Clinton** | **43. George W. Bush**

Took office	Jan 20 1989	Jan 20 1993	Jan 20 2001
Left office	Jan 20 1993	Jan 20 2001	—
Birthplace	Milton, MA	Hope, AR	New Haven, CT
Birth date	June 12 1924	Aug 19 1946	July 6 1946
Death date	—	—	

29. Warren G. Harding

Mar 4 1921

Aug 2 1923•

Blooming Grove, OH

Nov 21 1865

Aug 2 1923

30. Calvin Coolidge

Aug 2 1923

Mar 3 1929

Plymouth, VT

July 4 1872

Jan 5 1933

31. Herbert Hoover

Mar 4 1929

Mar 3 1933

West Branch, IA

Aug 10 1874

Oct 20 1964

32. Franklin D. Roosevelt

Mar 4 1933

Apr 12 1945•

Hyde Park, NY

Jan 30 1882

Apr 12 1945

37. Richard M. Nixon

Jan 20 1969

Aug 9 1974★

Yorba Linda, CA

Jan 9 1913

Apr 22 1994

38. Gerald R. Ford

Aug 9 1974

Jan 20 1977

Omaha, NE

July 14 1913

——

39. Jimmy Carter

Jan 20 1977

Jan 20 1981

Plains, GA

Oct 1 1924

——

40. Ronald Reagan

Jan 20 1981

Jan 20 1989

Tampico, IL

Feb 11 1911

——

• Indicates the president died while in office.

★ Richard Nixon resigned before his term expired.